METAPHYSICAL BALM

poems by Michèle Betty

People! Read Poetry

First published in Cape Town, South Africa by Dryad Press (Pty) Ltd in 2017

www.dryadpress.co.za

First edition, first printing, March, 2017

Second impression, 2018

Cover design and artwork by Ben Grib.

DTP and layout design by Imagnary House Publishers.

Printed and bound by Digital Action (Pty) Ltd.

The title text of this book is set in Hoefler Text TT (Regular).

The body text of this book is set in Adobe Garamond Pro (Regular).

CONTENTS

for Joan Hambidge

SECTION I

In my beginning is my end.

– T. S. Eliot, 'East Coker'

Owl's birthright

Owl orients to her air cell,
double bends her neck,
tucks beak, neatly,
under right wing,
thrusts head forward
to pierce the inner membrane.
With her egg tooth,
she pecks a thousand times,
turns in an oval egg,
counterclockwise,
squirms, struggles,
works feverishly,
until with vigorous shove,
she pips through the shell.
Wet and panting
she lies still, strength sapped.
Trembling and afraid,
Owl claws to rise:
thirsting for water,
with a silent scream,
she opens her beak,
to swallow rain.

Owl alights in the dell

Owl, cryptic of colour,
alights in the dell,
nestles in the nook of a holly tree:
one light ring encircling one dark ring,
a hundred fossil rings complete,
perched in its crook,
head clock, clock, clocking,
umber eyes blinking.

Owl peers all the way to the bath,
to the bird-shaped pool,
the Divine image of us,
trip, trip, tripping
along seven sandstone boulders,
wedged in lilting water
drawn from the icy springs
of an ancient aquifer.

A child bends,
drinks greedily from the pool.

Owl thirsts.

Owl is a witness to wild horses

They came at sunrise –
the second the orange globe
rose a half-moon on the horizon,
tingeing the sky
pale pink and the purple of bruises –
nickering and nuzzling,
nostrils flaring, muscles aquiver,
sweat trickling down sinewed legs;
all shades of white,
all shades of black,
all shades of brown,
moving in stillness
to pass beneath the mottled boughs
of Owl's saffron tree
(like the Word,
a pulsing, living expression
of love in unison);
and when they left in quiet,
Owl considered whether
they had ever been,
but their evidence was everywhere
and their scent,
earthy and wholesome,
enveloped her.

THE BAPTISM OF OWL

Owl journeys to sprinkle holy water
cupped from a grotto at Lourdes,
travels to India to float diyas
down the River Ganges,
pilgrims to Mecca to drink deeply
from the Well of Zamzam.
With an Inhalation, a single Breath,
she returns in rejoice to her dell,
reaches in ritual,
with striped legs cast out before her,
for the cool waters of the pond,
flushes the pale ochre
of her disc-shaped face,
twitches her ear tufts,
rinses under beating wings,
stamps her feet in the shallows of salvation,
twirls her head in liberation's delight,
immerses herself in the icy waters
of her Dell's spirit spring.

A Dove delicately descends:
"Owl, Beloved,
I am well pleased."

THE DISCIPLESHIP OF OWL

Owl had a vision
whilst peering through the dark:
a figure sprung from the fertile fingers
of a brazen Botticelli,
a virgin goddess, towering in full armour,
strength of Zeus, companion of heroes,
yet careful in wisdom,
beckoning with olive branch
from the depths of her golden chariot.
And in the instant Athena
focused her gaze,
Owl was compelled
to rest a cheek at her shoulder,
to hover with healing wings,
knowing, intuitively, that she,
like those Favoured Fishermen,
would abandon
everything she knew,
everyone she loved,
every comfort born of the nest,
to bask in the brilliance
of her vision's radiant light.

A SUPERNATURAL LONGING

Stirring from a mild slumber,
Owl longs for the olive-scented
breath of the wind.
As the first sign of light
overshadows the wild olive,
Owl senses the faithful falling
of an early-morning dew,
settling in the smooth
creases of her cheeks.
Surpassing all other desires,
Owl inhales the olive-scented
breath of the wind;
a supernatural breeze
stirs through the glade,
one-hundred-thousand leaves rustling,
reigning over her –
Animus
Pneuma
Ruh
Ruach.
Gripped by God,
Owl inhales
the cool breath of the spirit.

A TRANSVERBERATION OF THE HEART

Owl embarks on a detailed study
of the human body,
beginning in the cranial cavity
housing the skull and brain,
she traces a subtle ripple
through the cervical region
delicately enclosing the spinal cord,
navigating south toward the thoracic basin,
she journeys past the clavicles,
to bronchi, oesophagus, lymph nodes,
on to nerves,
twining into the pleural chamber
surrounding each lung,
to focus her gaze
on the pericardial plane,
heart of four chambers
enclosed in a triple-layered,
protective sac:
site of the transverberation
of Teresa of Ávila,
El Castillo Interior,
a crystal castle housing
seven interior courts,
emanating light,
recipient of consolations,
recurrent visions of angels,
a heart levitating in ecstasy,
pierced by the golden lance of a seraph,
left sweetly inflamed
by a mystical, divine love.

THE FORESIGHT OF OWL

Owl hoots three times
perched in the shadows
of an oversized moon;
a dusk duet resounds
before, with jerking head,
she stoops, swallows whole,
the spoils of a silent hunt.

SECTION II

The river is within us, the sea is all about us.
– T. S. Eliot, 'The Dry Salvages'

Owl encounters Crow

For forty days and forty nights
a storm raged through the dell.
Owl, weak and feeble, has not eaten.
As she swoops to the gloomy grey
of her saffron tree,
a sickly shadow passes overhead –
a reek of the ghost of Faustus.
Owl, transfixed,
peers through sullen light to see
Crow hunkering over Kill:
a glut of blood,
a mangle of bones.
He picks out the eye,
swallows and stares.
Black Eye meets White Eye.
As Crow's howl fills the glade,
lightning claps,
bearing rain in torrents.
Owl shudders,
and with eyes firmly closed,
flees in trepidation.

Owl confronts a crisis

Owl wrestles with a vindictive Crow
on a barren ledge of mountain
that ekes into a vortex,
a thousand metres above a turbulent sea.

She casts Crow off
with a fierceness that belies her body,
but in her eagerness to flee,
wedges the underside
of her claw in a crevice,
a pathway for cascading winter waterfalls.

For days she fights the clasp
of the stubborn rock,
but when rain pelts relentlessly,
she senses dereliction.

As days turn to nights,
water funnels through her eyes,
matts her feathers,
hail hammers her belly
and bruises her flank,
she begins to wonder
in her surreal state:

Can Owls drown?

In fury and frustration,
Owl's wings outstretch instinctively,
pulse to a quickened beat;
she relaxes her grip on the rock
and with a utopian exhale,
writhes to twist herself free.

Owl's angel

No evil shall befall you, nor shall affliction come near
your tent, for to His angels God has given command
about you, that they guard you in all your ways.

– Psalms 91 (10–12)

Owl made a choice
to travel to a new place.
She circled, airborne,
checked for Crow,
branched in the direction
of the flat mountain
and swooped silently
to the security
of a familiar yellowwood.
Braving new ground,
she circled up and over the treeline,
reached the mist of the mountain,
looped to penetrate and
experience new clarity,
but – looking down through
puffs of white cloud –
she was startled to
see Crow laughing
with menace from the entrance
of a darkened cave,
and, falling, she crashed through the
branches and needles of
a hundred stagnant pines,
stalling in the remnants
of the blister and bone
of a discarded animal carcass.
It was then,
a mystical creature,

hair coils of fiery bronze,
sword raised in right arm,
scooped Owl lightly up,
and transported her
with tender fervour
to the safety of her nest.

The Energy of Anatomy

Owl, bird with a four-chambered heart,
crimson in colour,
thumping 500 beats a minute,
aspect of her eyes
forward-facing and wizened,
with three-dimensional
binocular vision in monochrome,
a visible third eye,
nictitating for prolonged protection.

But, curiously,
the medulla, wedged in the brain
for triangular hearing,
surprises most:
95 000 neurons –
three times as many as Crow.

Owl and Crow converse

Make straight in the wasteland a highway for our God.
— Isaiah 40 (3)

There are Light Workers
declares Owl cryptically to Crow.
Light Workers,
Workers living in the Light,
self-reliant and headstrong,
a legion of old souls, auras of indigo,
floating across the orbit of your temples
like a cooling compress
infused with the fragrance of
geranium and jasmine.
Crow cocks his head dubiously to the side,
to numb the cauldron blazing in his head.

There is a New Brain
sighs Owl patiently to Crow.
A New Brain,
a Brain that is New,
independent, yet linked telepathically,
one in a trinity of brains,
millions of neurons per square inch,
transferring energy,
fed by spiritual mysteries –
every hair on your head is counted –
the mark of it, is Light.
Crow blinks, confused,
shakes out his feathers,
to calm the shudders
coursing through his flesh.

There are Earth Angels
muses Owl curiously to Crow.
Earth Angels,
Angels on the Earth
living amongst the spirit myths of Origen,
mystic and messianic,
with truth in their perception,
whose pilgrim purpose is Peace,
filling the God-shaped hole
in every discontented Heart
with a legacy of miracles,
a catalyst to heal the hurt.
Crow hunkers down to
hide his gnawing hunger,
swallows, and blinks at Owl.
Stupefied.

SECTION III

And what you do not know is the only thing you know
And what you own is what you do not own
And where you are is where you are not.

– T. S. Eliot, 'East Coker'

Caesura

for Jo

Owl pauses in a lull
at a windowpane of eight quadrants,
balances on the sill,
peers into dust-flecked light
lofting onto brick-brown parquet floors.
She observes the details
of a child's simple sketch:
oversized head and stick legs,
with a swirl of brilliant yellow and green,
lovingly framed in black ebony.
A pale-grey Weimaraner,
with blue eyes staring,
startles as it sits statuesque
in an oversized wingback chair.
On a nest of side tables,
an array of pills:
insomnia, anxiety, painkillers,
nausea, morphine.

Bits of Lego are strewn about.

Owl sits,
transfixed and immobile,
at the windowpane
of eight quadrants –
lets her wing feathers
splay across the moats of her eyes.

OWL AWAKES TO AN ILL OMEN

A darkening in Owl's plumage
was the first omen
of the onset of her ailment,
followed by the fleshy,
grape-like clusters
collecting at her wing joints,
the base of her beak,
then weight loss, coupled with
an insidious weakness –
a deep-set lethargy.

To curb the ill-fated spread,
Owl sought out a curative,
an overgrown grove
of her favourite trees:
Cunonia capensis,
butterspoon trees,
rooted in fertile earth
alongside a spirited stream.

She wrapped her talons
around the ash-coloured bark,
shuffled to gaze beyond stipules
of bronze butterspoons
at the panorama before her.
Inhaling the rarefied mountain air
(in the manner of Hans Castorp
ensconced at the Berghof),
time stood still,
her anxiety dissipated.
Liberated and consoled,
she waited in seclusion
for deliverance from demons,
enlightenment for her soul.

TRANSITIONS

for Marina

Can you live on another plane,
incarnate,
soul travel to a different dimension,
transmuted?

Can you edge out your physical pain,
in a metaphysical world?
Dare you message us through a medium,
shaken?

Are you beset by
ghouls and gargoyles,
beasts baring themselves
out of a fevered ferment?

Or, can you transition
effortlessly, through
a celestial light
towards a haven, heaven bound?

And, can you do all this, child,
lying wrapped in your percale cotton cocoon,
my hand lying heavy
on the nape of your fragile neck?

LA BÊTE NOIRE

In the palpable midnight gloom,
Owl shifts from one foot
to another,
shift, shift,
shift, shift,
eyes blink open, unbidden,
with a start,
an incurable vision
from the past, looms,
shift, shift
shift, shift.
Balancing precariously,
Owls' talons gouge
the forked branches
of her Corkwood –
a crimson resin oozes
over mottled bark.
As the musky scent of myrrh
overwhelms her,
Owl laments,
"Is there no balm
in Gilead?"

A PECULIAR ALIENATION

Owl pricks her ears
to attune to the scattered sounds
of a multitude of crickets clicking,
the late-afternoon cooing call of doves,
the trickle of water
over the sandstones of her dell,
the scurrying of ants
on the forest floor below.
In this background symphony,
she opens wide
the amphitheatre of her mind:
the beating of her bird heart quickens,
blood rushes to her pale face,
a discordant dizziness overcomes her
as she lifts her wings in an arc,
to contemplate, how it is,
that amongst all this profusion
she perches, without consolation,
so devastatingly alone.

Spiritual reflections from a fish tank

In a sprawling pet shop
an array of tropical fish
float in rectangular tanks
stacked high and wide,
fluorescent globes
distribute a melancholy glow,
seeping through crystalline water,
to reveal wide-open eyes
glaring from the shadows
cast by coral and willowy water plants.

On closer inspection,
to the shop owner's ambivalence,
several specimens appear
in the throes of a curious death dance –
an alien twist and loop by the parrotfish,
a neurotic, side-up, surface floating by the surgeonfish,
an unnatural gasping by the angelfish and, finally,
the paleontological mudskipper,
leaping with a repeated and doleful
head-banging against invisible glass.

A NARROW PLACE

Owl deliberates
as her down feathers diminish
and thicker juvenile ones,
drab in colour for camouflage,
metamorphose in contours,
across her rump and scapula.

Elevated on a terrace,
amongst tufts of luxuriant ferns,
she studies the shape
of the crevice where
she used to wedge herself in stealth –
a secret, arched alcove,
between the stratified sandstone opening
of two towering boulders.

As drops of vapour precipitate,
a melancholy call floats
along the delicate footpath,
winding its way
into the fertile river basin,
and descends through
the fissure of the valley:
a palliative resignation –
the nook, now a narrow place,
inaccessible, no longer a comfort
for the exercise of old rituals.

Seeking Sahasrana

for Fanini

Today
I wandered
the width
of my garden,
choosing only
white Selma Bock;
enlarged crowns
of whiter-than-white
agapanthus
with lilac-lavender centres;
one-thousand-
thousand petals,
stem
after evergreen stem,
until
not one remained,
to place
by your bedside,
a day
too late.

SECTION IV

Descend lower, descend only
Into the world of perpetual solitude
– T. S. Eliot, 'Burnt Norton'

Untergehen

Owl balances tirelessly, in solitude,
amongst the shallow, fluted branches
of a handsome corkwood tree,
nestles in the creamy-green
dense flower heads,
picks at seeds overflowing
from ovoid fruits.

She visualises the hunt:
a scan to scour and possess her prey,
a pull-back of her head.
Like the sun,
an over-rich star
dripping down to the horizon,
she swoops dangerously
to descend, silently weightless,
to the Underworld.
With a forward thrust of feet,
talons spread wide,
she overcomes her prey
with a magnanimous, yet sudden
snap of her beak.

A PRIEST'S JOURNEY

He walked upright,
a graceful gait,
clothed in black,
with a white collar,
a silver crucifix
pinned neatly to his lapel.
Like a *Ficus natalensis,*
he was deep-rooted,
boughs outstretched,
a dense evergreen shelter for
transient birds and bats.

It was only the beating,
like an excessive pruning out of season,
with no tender daub of salve applied,
that caused him to shudder unexpectedly.
Like a root ball shocked,
he lost his now wilted leaves.

Three men had pierced
his right side with a knife,
their fists drew scarlet welts
from under both eyes,
they held him down,
tied him up,
locked him away
and left him for dead.

And cloaked for hours
in that shroud of inky dark,
he scribbled letters,
on wafer-thin pages
torn from his Bible,
first to the ones he loved
and then to God.

A Russian fatalism

Owl stood transfixed
in the remnants of her nest,
shuddered at the sticks
and bits of bone
splayed about amongst
ruffled feathers and
an owlet's severed claw.
She hunkered down,
neck sinking into breast,
slowed her breath,
took no food,
and like a Russian Soldier
Lying Down in the Snow,
lay motionless in a perilous grave,
to blink occasionally at Crow
hopping annoyingly
on one leg,
to and fro,
to and fro,
before her steadfast gaze,
which clung to the memories
that flashed before her eyes –
lightning illuminating
a deafening darkness.

Owl's eyes

At the angle of Owl's eye,
beneath the lower lid
rests a membrane
extending horizontally
across the span of the eyeball,
separating lid from socket,
a third eye,
nictitating during night dreams
for heightened moisture
and increased visibility,
a microscopic and tenuous
three-layered epithelium
of translucent connective tissue –
a liminal zone
at the threshold.

An indivisible continuum

Owl watched, mesmerised
by the metallic blue-green
of the humpback salmon
moving stealthily to spawn
in the natal rivers of their birth,
pressed in their oblong hundreds,
simultaneously in shadow and iridescent light,
shimmering upstream against the current,
passing fingerlings migrating, tail first, downstream,
to estuaries feeding the open ocean,
depositing eggs in the gravel beds
of quiet pools at the base of falls and rapids,
then, calmly willing the water to flood their gills,
they alter to a silvery pale-grey,
transferring nutrients
rich in nitrogen, sulphur,
carbon and phosphorous
to adjacent riparian woodlands,
moving with the uncanny precision
of a mystical magnetoception,
toward the parabola of an imminent death
that draws them, tail first, downstream.

SECTION V

Between melting and freezing
The soul's sap quivers. There is no earth smell
Or smell of living thing. This is the spring time
But not in time's covenant.

– T. S Eliot, 'Little Gidding'

Owl invokes a paraclete

for Christopher Clohessey

Holy Spirit
Spirit of Truth
Lightful Spirit
Holy Breath
Almighty Breath
Giver of Life
Lord of Grace
Helper
Comforter
Counsellor
Supporter
Advocate
Paracletus
Parakletos
Paraclete
Who can you be?
What will you look like?
Grace infused
with virtue,
light to distil
dark corners,
tongues of fire
to empty a tomb.

ENTBINDUNG

In the tranquil stillness
of a womb,
at the moment of conception,
gametes combine to form
a gravitationally centred
unitary cell,
an embryo mantled
in warm water.
After a momentary lull,
a rapid division of cells
until on the fifteenth day
a primal midline uprises
to furrow a path
from what will be
coccyx and sacrum
enfolding on itself,
to the embryonic heart,
generating from the epiblast,
three germ layers shaping
bone and muscle, organs
and liquid crystalline connective tissue,
to form vertebrae and limb buds,
a neural tube, the brain, spinal cord,
nervous system, neural crest;
a bilateral symmetry
enveloped in two body-ness,
birthed from a primitive
primordial streak –
an entranced tracing
by the Finger of God.

INSCAPES

The iris of his almond eyes
alights on the daisies.
He hunches down,
checks his strap is
securely over his neck.
As slender fingers grip the zoom,
he raises the lens, slowly,
to an expectant face.
His tongue wets his lips,
words trip over his tongue.
Click, click.
Each white dot
flecked on a blood-orange petal,
where moments before
appeared as a pinprick,
now an elongated, tubular heart –
Scotus's *haecceitas*,
Hopkins' inscape,
and I stand back
in awe of Him.

OBSERVATIONS FROM THE TIDE WATERS

Owl surveys the vista
from her immutable perch
in an overgrown waterpear,
rooted in a squelchy sandbank
alongside undulating woodland
in the Great Zambezi basin.

The fishing boat's nose
decelerates through
a carpet cloud of rising mist,
parting like the Red Sea for Moses,
travels across metamorphic beds
fringed with igneous rock.

As the boat trawls through lapping waters,
a bright orange lure
is attached to strengthened line,
the ratchet is loosed and Owl's ears prick
with the plop of a cast into a current
streaming as constant as the call of the Creator.

A hippo bellows from the reeds below,
the line goes taut, the rod arcs a semicircle,
a metre-high leap of a tigerfish twisting in the air,
jerks off the three-pronged hook,
blue-orange tailfins blazing, silver-tipped scales
flashing the morning sun's reflection and the fish's fine
escape.

Owl yearns to abandon herself
to a tide so tumultuous.

WRAP YOUR HEAD AROUND YOUR HEART

whispered Owl,
to her owlets
swooping down
with Providence
from a secret perch,
fluting feathers
shifting sound energy,
silencing flight,
omniscient, as she hovers,
mantling her prey,
to feed them,
nesting in their theocracy,
for the tenth time that day,
twisting twirls of earthworm,
wriggling woes of
a mouse pounced.
Listen, murmured Owl
to her owlets –
wrap your head
around your heart.

Duende

no formar más que la médulla de forma

– Federico García Lorca

Owl felt the blood surge
from the knobbly soles
of her feathered feet
rushing up her sinewed legs,
ascending in a rhythmic tempo
to balloon in flexible arteries,
passing through hollow
cavities in her neck,
pooling in minute reservoirs
at the base of her head.
As she swivels her neck 270 degrees,
"Olé! Vive Dios!" exalts Owl,
listening to the stamping
of her feet, flamboyantly roused
by the curved sensation
of this unearthly, flame-coloured,
swell of blood.

BEYOND UNDERSTANDING

Und sie staunen dem krönlichen Haupt, das für immer,
schweigend, der Menschen Gesicht
auf die Waage der Sterne gelegt.

– Rainer Maria Rilke, 'Die Zehnte Elegie, Duino Elegies'

Owl peers through
a circular portal,
a chronology
two-thousand years
before the birth of Christ,
to an exuberant
Mesoamerican civilization
inhabiting the area from
Mexico through Belize,
Guatemala to Honduras,
a hieroglyphic language
depicted in stone *stelae*,
arithmetics and calendrics,
astronomical systems
encompassing labyrinths
to appreciate equinoxes,
lunar phases and seasons,
ceremonial architecture
with monumental palaces,
stepped pyramids and temples
trading cacao, salt and seashells,
jade and obsidian.

Owl peers again through
the circular portal
to laboratory scientists,
epigraphers and archaeologists
manipulating instruments

for Newton activation
and multispectral imaging,
dating a mysterious ceramic cylinder
painted with metaphors by the Maya:
a rain god's abundant paradise of
flowering orchards,
mystical sea creatures,
shadow, breath, blood and bone,
spook-like creatures,
violent stars.

Ancient giants

Coelacanth,
fish of rare lineage,
transitional species,
living fossil,
fish of eight fins,
a heart of variant shape,
bottle-green fish creation
crafted from clay,
extinct then
miraculously rediscovered –
like the Fisher of Men,
of David's fine line,
enigma both God and man,
reaching from the realms
of a church archaic,
twelve devoted disciples,
a heart of variant shape,
in a crooked cross immortalised,
now bidding from
amongst the pages
of a Bible plucked
from antiquity,
feeding five thousand
on a hackneyed hill
from a single
woven basket
filled with
fish and loaves.

Ancestral karma

The cedar tree,
abundant at altitude,
piniforous in nature,
stretched her boughs wide,
thick as ramparts,
a comfort for nesting
squirrels and birds,
her wood yielding *cedrium*,
eliciting a soothing fragrance –
dwelling place of Gilgamesh's gods,
prow and stern of Phoenician vessels,
wainscotted roof and floor
of King Solomon's Temple.

Owl rests in the shadows
of the cedar tree,
wraps herself in its warmth,
to survey the complexities of life,
surprising in their sharp agonies,
memento, homo, quia pulvis es,
dust unto dust,
a vita peracta –
redolent truths,
rediscovered amongst
the scent and sturdiness
of the cedarwood.

IN-SEEING AN OCEAN

Owl imagined for a day
that she was an ocean,
mile upon mile of weighted water,
refracted light and soundless shadows,
with enigmatic sea creatures suspended
like a foetus in the womb:
giant whales spurting
plumes of iridescent water,
multi-coloured luminous shoals,
salt-laden, frothy foam,
scalloped seashells
and a gravitational force
sparking warm currents
and the soothing pressure of tides,
emanating from the god-like
face of the moon.

Owl's alchemy

I *Nigredo*

In the shadow of
somnambulant gardens
sloping down to Lake Zurich,
at the heart of the home of
the wizard of Küsnacht,
Owl collects chemicals
for an arcane experiment:
prima materia,
lead and tin,
copper and iron,
tumbles them together
to form a Black Mass
to be calcinated, putrefied,
washed to purify and
then carefully distilled.

II *Albedo*

Concealed amongst
acres of woodlands,
reading in reverie,
The Secret of the Golden Flower,
Owl rescues her retort stand,
regulates the blue-rimmed flame
emanating from the burner.
"Hieros gamos," she whispers –
a synthesis of opposites –
and across the span
of the lead-like mass,
Owl achieves the sheen
of a vast Whitening.

III *Rubredo*

Following a circuitous route,
Owl comes to rest in the forests
at the Villa Eranos,
takes in a breath,
unlocks the retort stand
to reveal a crystallised stone:
gold, but not the common gold,
radiating the red
of a cosmic healing,
Lapis Philosophorum –
The Philosopher's Stone.

ODE TO ZARATHUSTRA

'Zarathustra,' intuits Owl,
an orator preaching parables
amidst the pathways
of dense trees and
flighty families of birds.

'Zarathustra,' wills Owl,
offering alms to salvage
the forest from its malaise –
her thoughts flashing
an ellipsis, birthed in
the recesses of her
instinctive animal brain.

'Zarathustra,' incarnates Owl,
in a breath borne
of the Dionysian –
a vision of eternal return
from an uncreative crisis
to the myth-making power
of a Carpenter offering
a communion of bread and wine,
until forced, on bended knee,
to hoist a human-sized
wooden cross.

VISITATION

What remains of the self unwinds and unwinds, for none
Of the boundaries holds
- Mark Strand, 'In Memory Of Joseph Brodsky'

Last night as I stood
white-knuckled, clutching
the edges of my moon-shaped basin,
purple lips of a puffer fish,
silver-scaled and goggle-eyed,
I saw Dennis.
There he hovered,
unafraid and observant,
bone thin, in a fine grey flannel,
deep maroon shirt,
top two buttons casually undone,
curling grey-black hair
ruffling through the shirt holes,
shiny black brogues laced
and those eyes, near black,
twinkling at my fishbowl face.
Not a man of many words,
"Hmmm," he said, "Hmmm,"
with lips lightly upturned,
he leaned toward me,
an overwhelming comfort.

To Circumnavigate an Archipelago

From an anomalous volcanic hotspot,
molten magma upwells,
to form thermal mantle plumes,
tectonic plates in motion
create continental fragments
with vast underwater islands,
seamounts and circular atolls
accompanying shallows,
banks and ancient reefs,
home to sea turtles and starfish,
bottlenose dolphins and speckled whale shark.

Owl circumnavigates,
soaring against gravity,
feather and hollow bone,
in rising lukewarm thermals,
weight, lift, drag, thrust –
from island to separate island,
from azure to blue-black sea –
each port of call a unique narrative,
providing a new perspective
on the archipelago
that first appeared
in an exotic, vivid vision.

SECTION VI

After the kingfisher's wing
Has answered light to light, and is silent, the light is still.
At the still point of the turning world.

– T. S Eliot, 'Burnt Norton'

The wingspan of my Owl

The day I huffed
up the lopsided steps,
sawn from the bark rings
of an old oak tree,
to the top of the sloping hillside
behind my house,
mind as dense with scepticism
as the Doubting Disciple,
was the day I saw that Owl.

That day,
I could not see
for the looking down,
for the muffled mist
playing tricks with my eyes.
Yet, peering through
the dense treeline,
it appeared,
hovering effortlessly,
in the forward motion of a sunbird:
the largest Owl I had ever seen,
talons gripping the underside
of the massive branches
of a gnarled oak,
sharpened beak scraping
at sweetened shards of bark,
wingspan reaching
from fingertip to fingertip
of outstretched human arms,
the flapping more a thudding,
as if to say,
How can you doubt?
How do you dare?

ACCEPTANCE

Across the expanse
of a twilight sky,
a Sickle Moon
and the Evening Star,
Owl discerns mist
collecting resplendent
in humid air,
weightless as the down
feathers of her youth,
dispersing enigmatically
to settle in solitude,
refracted and reflected,
in puffs and pockets,
on each and every
shadow touched.

As I raised my eyes heavenward

I

In the year I turned forty
an ache birthed itself
in my hip.
Slowly, it gravitated inward
from my soft inner thigh,
creeping snakelike,
to grasp for my groin,
twisting selfishly
around my hip bone,
waiting for protest.

I paid it no attention,
deferred to it demurely,
but its grip on me only tightened.
I felt the ache travel,
down my tibia,
into my cruciate,
sidle along my calf muscle,
with a stab in the lower back,
to arrest resistance.

I dabbled with many devices:
tablets round as a moon eclipsed,
vials red and green,
yoga more often
or sometimes less,
undignified dressing
and undressing for
medical muses of all sorts.
But the devil held me fast.

II

So, I visited a church
to voice my disapproval
to the Three Persons in one God.
The priest relayed a tale
of a Mexican child,
scalded but then healed
as she nestled unseen
at the altar of the Divine.
Diligently, I prayed.
But the devil held me fast.

III

Months later,
I sojourned the streets of London,
searching for a cross,
a haven for an hour.
Amongst scaffolding secluded,
I came upon the church,
russet-red stained-glass windows
depicting the passion
along the length and breadth
of its ancient walls,
hundreds of tea-light candles burning.

An old man appeared earnestly before me,
grey, curling eyebrows,
lips gently lifted,
eyes softly sparkling.
'I cannot,' I explained wryly,
'I am not trained.'

I reached to touch the tassels on his cloak.
He insisted,
waved away my veiled insecurity.
'Have courage.'
He insisted.

So I stood on the altar,
with my accompanying ache,
gravitating from my soft inner thigh,
to grasp for my groin,
twisting around my hip bone,
travelling down my tibia,
into my cruciate,
sidling along my calf muscle,
with a stab in my lower back
and I offered the chalice
as he raised the host,
fingers trembling,
'This is the Blood of Christ.'

'You must wipe,'
whispered a raven-haired woman
'the chalice,'
and so I did.
'The Blood of Christ'
wipe,
'The Blood of Christ'
wipe,
and I whispered to the Divine
for intercession,
I argued with Him for healing.

IV

But when I sat serenely
on the wooden bench,
my feet earthed
on the reddened pile carpet,
duties complete,
I felt the familiar pain
splinter in my back,
and water collected in the corners
of my eyes – from the pain
you understand.
My hands were shaking.

V

In the year I turned forty,
I resolved to walk in London,
early, before my loved ones woke.
I slipped out,
breathed in the misty air,
checked my map for directions,
from Regent's Park into the
Queen Mary's Gardens.
I passed the Royal Institute of Architects,
turned left into Park Square,
and left to the Outer Circle,
where I was arrested
by the rows of delphiniums,
begonias, foxgloves,
snowdrops, snapdragons.

As I raised my eyes heavenward

I crossed the York Bridge,
ambled towards the Inner Circle,
anointed by a sight that could soften
even the deepest of aches –
twelve-thousand roses,
travelling up trellises,
scrambling along loamy soil,
every colour reflected,
buds aflame
hearts heaven bound,
some as white as my linen folding cloth,
others as golden as my chalice,
still others as blood red
as the wine I had offered.
As I raised my eyes heavenward
and listened to my feet crunch the gravel,
I knew, startled and with a clarity
reserved for the righteous,
that my deep ache had left me,
whilst walking.

Acknowledgements

This collection was conceived in partial fulfilment of the requirements of a Masters in Creative Writing, completed at the University of Cape Town in 2015. I wish to thank the university and my lecturers and in particular my mentor and supervisor Joan Hambidge for her invaluable guidance and support.

I would also like to thank Douglas Reid Skinner of *Stanzas* and Finuala Dowling of *Aerodrome*, who selected some of the poems from this collection for publication in *Stanzas* and *Aerodrome* respectively, as follows:

'An indivisible continuum', 'Duende' and 'Observations from the tide waters', in *Stanzas*; 'Seeking Sahasrana', on *Aerodrome*; 'Visitation' and 'Transitions', in *Stanzas*.

Extracts from the poems 'East Coker', 'Little Gidding', 'The Dry Salvages' and 'Burnt Norton' are from: *Four Quartets* by T.S. Eliot (London: Faber & Faber Ltd, 1966) and are reprinted with the generous permission of Faber and Faber Ltd and © The Estate of T.S. Eliot.

— Michèle Betty